PACIFIC NORTHWEST BALLET *Presents*

Nutcracker

Choreography by KENT STOWELL

Costume & Set Design by MAURICE SENDAK

Photography by ANGELA STERLING

Introduction by FRANCIA RUSSELL

SASQUATCH BOOKS
SEATTLE

©2005 by Pacific Northwest Ballet Association
All rights reserved. No portion of this book may be reproduced
or utilized in any form, or by any electronic, mechanical,
or other means without the prior written permission of the publisher.

Printed in China
Published by Sasquatch Books
Distributed by Publishers Group West
10 09 08 07 06 05   6 5 4 3 2 1

Photographs by Angela Sterling
Book design by Kate Basart

Library of Congress Cataloging-in-Publication Data is available.
ISBN: 1-57061-469-5

Sasquatch Books
119 South Main Street, Suite 400
Seattle, WA 98104
(206) 467-4300
www.sasquatchbooks.com
custserv@sasquatchbooks.com

Hoffman, Tchaikovsky, and Petipa, a stellar trio if ever there was one, but who could have predicted the enduring popularity of their *Nutcracker*? There are many reasons for a success lasting well over a hundred years, and surely the beauty of the score and the prominence of Christmas in the story are at the top of the list. Whatever the explanation, it is clear that *Nutcracker* has become an indispensable part of the American family's holiday season.

The ballet, created in 1891 by the great choreographer Marius Petipa, bore curiously little relationship to the story of E. T. A Hoffman on which it was based. Hoffman's rich, bizarre tale had been watered-down out of recognition and was a great disappointment to Tchaikovsky, whose score retained the dark overtones of the original. Literally countless versions of the *Nutcracker* have been produced over the years and most, whether using the Petipa choreography or not, have been faithful to his scenario.

When Kent Stowell decided to create his own *Nutcracker* for Pacific Northwest Ballet, my first thought was that it should be designed by Maurice Sendak, the celebrated children's book author and illustrator and the hero of our young family. The very predictability of the idea was Maurice's great objection when Kent contacted him, but he did agree to a meeting. The two future collaborators were immediately in unison as they compared their devotion to Hoffman and Tchaikovsky and so it took only one visit to a Pacific Northwest Ballet rehearsal for Maurice to fall in love with the company and the project.

With two fertile creative imaginations at work, completely in sync and at the same time paying homage to their artistic forbears, it is no surprise that the Stowell/Sendak production is not "just another *Nutcracker*," but richer and darker and with a spotlight trained on the private world of childhood. Their heroine, Clara, is the focal point for the entire ballet, and it is her story of preadolescent awakening that ties the many colorful scenes and divertissements together into a dramatically powerful whole.

How long will the appeal of even the greatest *Nutcracker* production last? Of course it is impossible to predict, but as long as ecstatic audiences continue to dance out of the theater year after year, one can safely say the *Nutcracker* phenomenon is still at its zenith. A work of art that mirrors the fears and joys of childhood; that combines drama, music, dance, and design in a wealth of color and variety; and that brings families together in celebration is surely deserving of immortality.

—FRANCIA RUSSELL
Pacific Northwest Ballet Artistic Director

Introduction

Curtain

Music by P. I. TCHAIKOVSKY
Choreography by KENT STOWELL
Sets & Costumes by MAURICE SENDAK
Lighting Design by RANDALL G. CHIARELLI

PROLOGUE

Many years ago in the German town of Nuremburg, a young girl named Clara lived with her brother, Fritz, and their parents, Dr. and Frau Stahlbaum. As our story opens, it is late afternoon on Christmas Eve and Clara has fallen asleep in her room. In a dream, her mysterious godfather, Herr Drosselmeier, appears and presents three small figures that act out a frightening story. A Nutcracker is seen defending the lovely Princess Pirlipat from the advances of a Mouse King. As brave as he is, the Nutcracker is defeated by the wicked Mouse King, who bites Pirlipat, changing her into an ugly monster. Clara is startled from her dream. Her nurse rushes in to help her dress for the Christmas party, which has already started.

ACT I
SCENE 1

The living room is filled with warmth and merriment as the Stahlbaum family welcomes relatives and friends to their annual Christmas festivities. Clara comes downstairs to join the party only to be confronted by a vision of giant mice. Frightened, she brushes away the memories of her dream and runs into her mother's arms. She is drawn into the happy celebration and the party continues until Herr Drosselmeier suddenly appears.

Godfather Drosselmeier is well known to all the children of Nuremburg. Despite his odd manner and appearance, he is a great favorite in the Stahlbaum home because he always brings surprises. This time, however, Clara is a little afraid of her godfather because of his strange role in her dream. Annoyed by Clara's shyness, Herr Drosselmeier gives Fritz a Mouse King doll and encourages him to tease Clara and disrupt the party. Then, to entertain all the guests, he presents two life-sized dancing dolls, a beautiful young ballerina and an Eastern sword dancer. Clara is fascinated by the ballerina doll and tries to persuade her godfather to give it to her. He refuses and instead produces three figures who reenact Clara's nightmare in a masque. Now Clara is truly frightened and would run away if her amazing godfather did not conjure up another surprise: a wooden Nutcracker. Clara is enchanted with the present and dances happily until her mischievous little brother, Fritz, grabs the doll and breaks it. The children's godfather steps in once more to bandage the wounded Nutcracker with his handkerchief and to dry Clara's tears.

As the evening draws to a close, Dr. Stahlbaum invites everyone, even the smallest children, to join in one last dance. Slowly the guests depart and Clara and Fritz are led off to bed.

SCENE 2

After the Stahlbaum family goes to bed, the resident mice make themselves at home in the living room. The first to appear are two baby mice, followed by their mother. Clara enters, looking for her Nutcracker, and accidentally trips over one of the baby mice. Mother Mouse runs off in a panic to call the other mice.

Suddenly, all the familiar objects in the room begin to change. The toy cabinet and living room furniture grow bigger and bigger, and the Christmas tree assumes nightmarish proportions. Out of a huge jack-in-the-box pops a Nutcracker, followed by an army of toy soldiers who line up to face the ragamuffin band of mice. At the climax of the battle, the Nutcracker fights a duel with a gigantic Mouse King. Seeing that the Nutcracker is about to be defeated, Clara bravely runs to his aid and magically kills the Mouse King with her shoe.

Scene 3

Clara is transformed into the beautiful young woman of her fantasies and, where the Nutcracker fell, a handsome prince appears. Together they walk from the Stahlbaum living room out into the Land of Snow. There Clara and her Prince dance together, joined by swirling flurries of snowflakes.

ACT II
Scene 1

Clara and the Prince are aboard a golden boat, sailing through visions of a magical land. They dock at an exotic port where they are greeted by the kingdom's Grand Pasha and his entourage. Clara notices that the Pasha looks suspiciously like her Godfather Drosselmeier. The Prince tells the story of the battle between the Nutcracker and his soldiers and the army of mice. Clara is praised for her bravery in saving the Nutcracker.

The Pasha, as Master of Ceremonies, brings on one group of dancers after another to entertain his honored guests. They see Moorish couples, a brilliant peacock in a gold cage, a Chinese tiger and his attendants, whirling dervishes, three *commedia dell'arte* characters, a spirited dance performed by four tiny couples, and a waltz danced by girls dressed in the colors of spring flowers. For their new friends, Clara and the Prince dance a romantic *pas de deux*, expressing their young love. All the Pasha's entertainers join them in a grand finale. At the height of the festivities the golden boat returns. It is time for Clara and the Prince to continue on their journey. Clara is reluctant to leave and, as she hesitates, the Pasha sends the boat on without her.

Scene 2

The magic kingdom fades and our story ends, as it began, with Clara on her bed in her own room, wondering where fantasy ends and growing up begins.

—*Francia Russell*

Program Notes

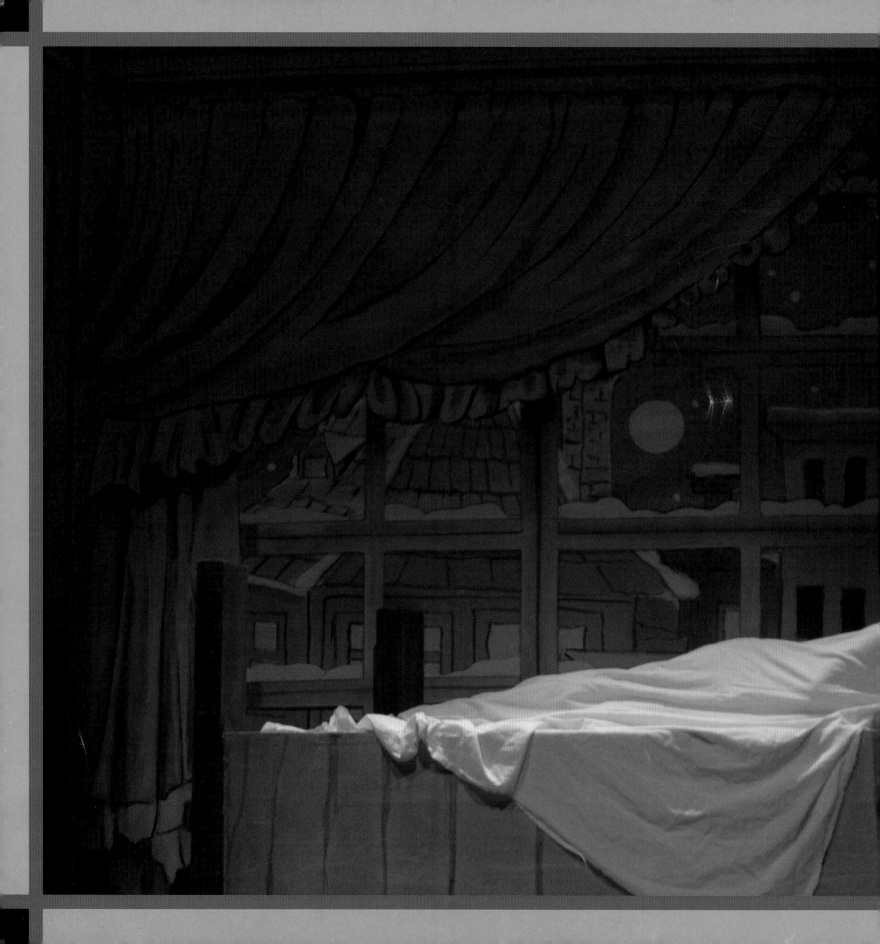

Prologue:
Clara's Bedroom

Clara couldn't wait for Mother and Father's Christmas Eve party tonight. All her friends and neighbors would be present, and there would be dancing and games and gifts. Not wanting to be tired for the party, she decides to take a short nap. Clara soon falls asleep and dreams of her beloved Godfather Drosselmeier.

In her dream, Godfather Drosselmeier gives Clara three dancers: a young princess named Pirlipat, a magical Nutcracker, and a scary Mouse King. At first Pirlipat enjoys dancing with both the Nutcracker and the Mouse King, but soon she grows wary of him and begins to dance only with the Nutcracker. This upsets the Mouse King greatly.

Godfather Drosselmeier, seeing the Mouse King upset, whispers something in his ear. Clara wonders, what could Drosselmeier be saying?

Then Godfather Drosselmeier and the Mouse King break up Pirlipat and the Nutcracker's dance. The Mouse King, while fighting with the Nutcracker, turns and bites Pirlipat. Instantly, she turns into an ugly monster. Frightened, Clara awakes from her nightmare and is surprised to hear music downstairs. The party has already begun!

Act 1: The Christmas Eve Party

Mother and Father are thrilled that their party is such a success. Children and their parents have gathered around the adorned Christmas tree and are dancing. But where is Clara?

At that moment, Clara enters the room, excited but sorry to be so late. Seeing Father and Mother, she runs to them and apologizes. Her friends soon join her and ask her to dance with them.

Suddenly, with a flash, Godfather Drosselmeier enters the party, bringing with him a bag full of gifts. Clara remembers her dream and is too frightened to greet her godfather.

Clara's annoying little brother Fritz, however, is not afraid of the new guest. Seeing Fritz come near him, Drosselmeier pulls out a toy Mouse King, much to Clara's dismay. Fritz calls to the boys to come join him, and they begin to play with his new toy.

Seeing Clara with her friends, Godfather Drosselmeier, with a wink of his eye and a flash of light, presents Clara with a life-sized ballerina doll. Clara and her friends marvel at the beautiful ballerina and her pretty costume. Then to their surprise the doll springs to life and dances around the party guests.

The boys yawn, bored by the ballerina. Godfather Drosselmeier then turns to them and in another flash presents a sword dancer.

The sword dancer leaps in the air and thrusts his saber.
The boys watch with wide eyes as the sword dancer continues his fight.

By then, the dinner bell had rung, and the guests depart for the dining room. Godfather Drosselmeier stops Clara to give her a special gift. Three masked dancers appear: Pirlipat, the Nutcracker, and the Mouse King— the same dancers from her dream! Clara watches, frightened, as her nightmare is reenacted.

Godfather

Drosselmeier sees that the dancers upset Clara. Dismissing the dancers, he comforts Clara and gives her a beautiful Nutcracker doll.

Clara instantly adores her new doll and dances with it as if it were a prince at a grand ball. She does not even notice that dinner has ended and the party guests have returned to the living room.

Seeing his sister so happy, Fritz snatches the Nutcracker from Clara. Grabbing the sword from the sword dancer, he throws the toy Nutcracker to the floor and stabs it, causing it to break. Upset that her favorite new toy is damaged, Clara clutches the Nutcracker in her arms.

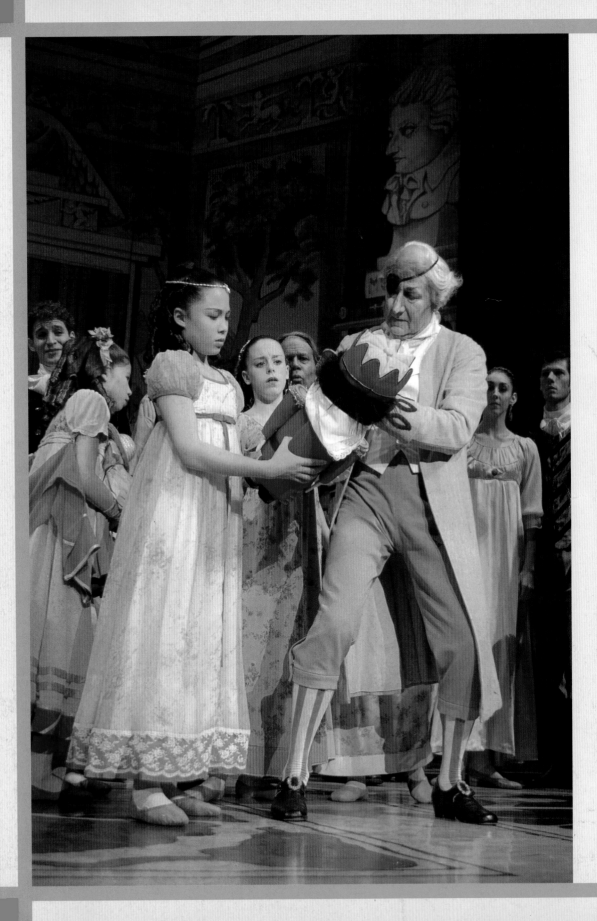

Godfather

Drosselmeier rushes forward, pulling out a white handkerchief and wrapping it around the broken doll as a bandage. Clara thanks her godfather. How could she have been so frightened of him before?

Trusting her godfather once again, she asks him to join her in a dance.

Just as their dance is about to end, Godfather Drosselmeier suddenly turns, grabs his coat, and dashes off in a hurry. With that, the party ends, and Clara watches sadly as the guests depart.

Act 1: The Living Room at Night

Later that night, Clara cannot sleep. Wanting her new Nutcracker, Clara realizes she left it in the living room under the tree. She creeps back into the living room, not wanting to wake up Mother and Father—and not noticing that two young mice are playing a game of patty-cake on the floor.

As Clara tries to find her way in the dark, she trips on a boy mouse. As the mouse cries, his mother rushes out and sees that Clara has hurt her child. The mouse mother begins to yell at Clara, scaring her.

As Mother Mouse continues to yell, Clara feels an odd sensation overcome her and the room begins to change. Everything becomes larger and more frightening. Suddenly, a giant mouse soldier jumps out from behind a corner, brandishing a sword.

The mouse soldier threatens Clara, and soon other mice join him. Clara, frightened by the soldier mice, runs around the now enormous Christmas tree looking for somewhere to hide. From behind a huge jack-in-the-box steps her new toy Nutcracker, now taller than she.

With a wave of his swa sword, the Nutcracker gives out a quick shout and is soon joined by a troop of toy soldiers.

Clara watches as troops of soldiers appear from behind the tree. Some march out with bayonets. Others have cannons. Some are even on horseback.

As the soldiers line up at attention, Clara walks around and inspects the troops, knowing that they are going to battle to defend her.

Then Attila, the mouse general, reappears, leading his soldier mice forward. The battle has begun, as toy soldiers tally forth against the mice rebels.

Already frightened by the battle around her, Clara becomes even more afraid as the largest mouse she has ever seen fills the room and surrounds the enormous Christmas tree. It is the Mouse King!

Attila and the Nutcracker begin to duel. Clara, scared by the giant mouse, takes off one of her shoes and throws it at the Mouse King, hitting him on the head and magically killing him. As he lay dying, smoke erupts from the Mouse King's body. Toy soldiers and mice run from the toxic room, and Clara, grabbing the handkerchief that once bandaged the Nutcracker, runs through a hole in the wall that leads to the outside world.

Act 1: The Land of Snow

Outside, in a landscape filled with snow, the Nutcracker, now transformed into a handsome Prince, steps into the moonlight and sees that the spell he was under has broken. He spies a huddled form under a white blanket. Whisking away the blanket, he is startled to find underneath a beautiful woman.

It is Clara! She too has been transformed and now steps forward as the beautiful woman she had always dreamed of becoming.

Free from the mice and in a magical fantasyland, Clara and her Nutcracker Prince dance together for what seems an eternity. At the close of their dance, the Prince tells Clara of his magical kingdom, and hand in hand, they start their journey toward it.

As the couple departs, a whirling storm of lady snowflakes flutters in, and with each passing snowflake the storm evokes a stirring dance.

As the snowstorm dance reaches an end, Clara and the Nutcracker board a majestic ship, looking back at the blustery landscape they are leaving behind.

Act 2: The Prince's Kingdom

After a long journey, Clara and her Prince land at his magical kingdom. They are welcomed by a group of children, mouse servants, and the Grand Pasha.

As the Pasha greets the couple, Clara can't help but think she's seen him before.

It is now Clara's turn to greet her hosts. Dressed like Godfather Drosselmeier's life-sized toy ballerina, she performs a solo dance for her greeters.

As Clara continues to dance the Prince steps in. Together they retell the story of their battle with the Mouse King and his soldiers. The story ends with how Clara saved the day and killed the evil Mouse King.

As their dance ends, the Pasha invites his guests to sit down. He has prepared for them an evening of entertainment.

Sitting in the seats of honor, Clara and the Prince watch as a group of Moorish dancers are the first to entertain them.

Next, a colorful peacock is brought out, carried in a large cage. Once released, the peacock performs a slow, exotic dance.

A Chinese tiger is led out to the stage by four attendants. As the tiger frolics about, the attendants keep him on leash. When finished, a man pops out of the tiger's head; it was only a costume!

Then, three whirling dervishes leap to the stage, performing a rousing dance as they fly through the air.

After the dervishes, three clownlike masked and colorful figures perform a spirited Italian performance known as *commedia dell'arte*.

A dollhouse is then brought forward, and out pop four childlike couples who greet their audience.

In the final entertainment, a flower maiden steps forward and begins a solo dance.

The flower maiden is joined by other colorful spring flowers as her dance reaches its peak.

Thankful to the Pasha for such grand entertainment, Clara and the Prince treat him and the kingdom to a romantic duet known as a *pas de deux*.

As Clara and her Prince conclude their *pas de deux*, they are joined by all the dancers of the evening in a grand finale.

But as the music stops the prince and dancers retreat. Curious, Clara approaches the remaining Pasha, who takes off his turban. He is really Godfather Drosselmeier! Clara is so terrified she awakes in her bed. It was only a dream! She wonders what truth her dreams of growing up may hold.

Artistic Directors

Kent Stowell – Godfather Drosselmeier
and Pasha
Francia Russell

Principals

Patricia Barker
Batkhurel Bold
Carrie Imler – Flora
Ariana Lallone
Christophe Maraval
Stanko Milov
Louise Nadeau
Kaori Nakamura
Noelani Pantastico
Jeffrey Stanton
Olivier Wevers
Le Yin

Soloists

Oleg Gorboulev – Dr. Stahlbaum
Casey Herd – Nutcracker Prince
Jonathan Porretta
Jodie Thomas
Mara Vinson – Adult Clara

Corps de Ballet

Nicholas Ade
Alison Basford
Kari Brunson
Maria Chapman – Frau Stahlbaum and
Peacock
Karel Cruz – Attila
Lindsi Dec
Chalnessa Eames
Rachel Foster – Ballerina Doll
Kiyon Gaines – Warrior Nutcracker
Laura Gilbreath
Taurean Green
Rebecca Johnston
Barry Kerollis
Kylee Kitchens
Stacy Lowenberg
James Moore
Jordan Pacitti – Sword Doll
Lucien Postlewaite
Lesley Rausch
Brittany Reid
Josh Spell
Kara Zimmerman

Apprentices

Jessika Anspach
Brennan Boyer
Erin Lewis
Sean Whiteman

PNB School Students

Kirra Steinbrueck – Young Clara
Jordan Veit – Fritz

Pacific Northwest Ballet

Contributor Biographies

Kent Stowell served Pacific Northwest Ballet as Artistic Director from 1977 to 2005. He began his dance training with Willam Christensen, later joining San Francisco Ballet and New York City Ballet. In 1970, he joined the Munich Opera Ballet as a leading dancer and choreographer and in 1975 was appointed Artistic Director of Frankfurt Ballet. He and his wife Francia Russell were named Artistic Directors of Pacific Northwest Ballet in 1977. His vast contributions to PNB's repertoire include *Nutcracker*, *Swan Lake*, *Cinderella*, *Carmina Burana*, *The Tragedy of Romeo and Juliet*, *Silver Lining* and *Firebird*.

Francia Russell was Pacific Northwest Ballet's Artistic Director and Director of the School from 1977 to 2005. Ms. Russell joined New York City Ballet in 1956 and was promoted to soloist in 1959; she danced with Jerome Robbins' Ballets USA for a year after her retirement. George Balanchine appointed her ballet mistress of the New York City Ballet in 1964. Ms. Russell has staged more than 100 of his ballets throughout the world. She and her husband Kent Stowell were named Artistic Directors of Frankfurt Ballet in 1975 and of Pacific Northwest Ballet in 1977.

Maurice Sendak is lauded as one of the world's most respected children's book artists. He has illustrated more than 78 books, many of which he authored. His work on Pacific Northwest Ballet's *Nutcracker* made the production a holiday tradition in the Northwest and unique among hundreds of Nutcracker productions. Many of the set and costume designs were used as illustrations in the 1984 book *Nutcracker*, by Crown Publishers. Mr. Sendak has also designed the sets for Houston Opera's *The Magic Flute*, New York Opera's *The Cunning Little Vixen*, Glyndebourne Opera's *The Love for Three Oranges,* and most recently, Chicago Opera Theater's *Brundibar*.

Angela Sterling was a soloist dancer with Pacific Northwest Ballet until a career ending back injury inspired her to pursue her second passion, photography. Knowing instinctively what moments to shoot, her work showcases the unique talents of the dancers she photographs. Her photography is seen regularly at Pacific Northwest Ballet, Ballet Les Ballet de Monte Carlo, Boston Ballet and Dutch National Ballet, as well as in *Dance Magazine*, *Pointe Magazine*, and many European dance magazines.

Pacific Northwest Ballet was founded in 1972 and was under the Artistic Directorship of Kent Stowell and Francia Russell from 1977 until their retirement in 2005. Under their direction, PNB became one of the largest and most highly regarded ballet companies in the United States, presenting over 90 performances a year at home in Seattle, Washington, and on tour. Pacific Northwest Ballet School, under the direction of Francia Russell, is recognized nationally as a leader in ballet training. In 2005, Peter Boal, former principal dancer with New York City Ballet, assumed the Artistic Directorship of Pacific Northwest Ballet.